Copyright © 2012 by Trivium Test Prep

ALL RIGHTS RESERVED. By purchase of this book, you have been licensed one copy for personal use only. No part of this work may be reproduced, redistributed, or used in any form or by any means without prior written permission of the publisher and copyright owner.

Trivium Test Prep is not affiliated with or endorsed by any testing organization and does not own or claim ownership of any trademarks, specifically for the EXPLORE exam. All test names (or their acronyms) are trademarks of their respective owners. This study guide is for general information and does not claim endorsement by any third party.

Printed in the United States of America

Table of Contents

Introduction 7

Chapter 1: The English Section 11
   Test Your Knowledge: The English Section 13
   Answers 25

Chapter 2: The Math Section 27
   Test Your Knowledge: The Math Section 45
   Answers 50

Chapter 3: The Reading Section 51
   Test Your Knowledge: The Reading Section 57
   Answers 60

Chapter 4: The Science Reasoning Section 61
   Test Your Knowledge: The Science Reasoning Section 64
   Answers 70

Final Thoughts 71

Introduction

The fact that you've purchased this book means two things. The first: You're preparing for, or at least considering, the EXPLORE exam. The second: You've already made an excellent first step in picking up this study guide.

We'll provide you with a detailed overview of the EXPLORE, so that you know exactly what to expect on test day. We'll also cover all of the subjects over which you will be tested, as well as provide multiple practice sections for you to test your knowledge and improve. No worries – even if it's been a while since your last major examination, we'll make sure you're more than ready!

What is the EXPLORE?

The EXPLORE exam by ACT, Inc. essentially follows the same format as its big brother, the ACT, which you will take in high school. Of course, this exam is smaller – it does not contain an essay section, and the material tested covers subjects only through the 8th-grade level.

The ACT is an important exam for college application. The EXPLORE serves as a great way for you to prepare for the ACT, which can maximize your ACT score. The EXPLORE also has a more immediate use as well – it indicates the level of your skills and knowledge, which will help you plan your high school coursework with efficiency.

Breaking Down the EXPLORE Exam

You will have 30 minutes for each of the separate sections on the EXPLORE exam. Those sections are:

- **English**
    - 40 Questions: Tests knowledge of grammar and usage.

- **Math**
    - 30 Questions: Tests knowledge of math (pre-algebra, algebra, etc.)

- **Reading**
    - 30 Questions: Tests reading comprehension through questions over multiple passages.

- **Science**
    - 28 Questions: Tests your fundamental knowledge and ability to understand science-related information.

Scoring

After you've completed the exam, you will receive a score from 1 – 25, with 1 being the lowest and 25 being the highest.

Each section (English, Math, Reading, and Science) will receive such a score, with a graph beside them indicating how well that score compares to those of other test takers across the country. This will help you understand your strengths and weakness, where you stand in relation to your classmates, and where you need improvement.

You cannot "pass" or "fail" the EXPLORE. Instead, your four scores for the individual sections will be averaged together into one "Composite" score. You also do not receive a penalty for selecting an incorrect answer, which means that you must be sure to **answer EVERY SINGLE QUESTION on EVERY SECTION.** Even if you are running out of time and don't even read the question, mark an answer choice! You have a chance of getting it correct and gaining a point!

How This Book Works

The subsequent chapters in this book are divided into a review of those topics covered on the exam. This is not to "teach" or "re-teach" you these concepts – there is no way to cram all of that material into one book! Instead, we are going to help you recall all of the information which you've already learned. Even more importantly, we'll show you how to apply that knowledge.

Each chapter includes an extensive review, with practice drills at the end to test your knowledge. With time, practice, and determination, you'll be well-prepared for test day.

LET'S MAKE A PLAN

Your score depends upon your making a solid study plan. Opening up practice questions and just jumping in won't help. You need to review the material, find your strengths and weaknesses, so that you know where to focus your time. Practice tests will come later.

Your Study Plan

> Schedule Study Time: Schedule when you will study each day and stick to it. If you have a specific amount of time set aside to work on preparing yourself, you won't have the added stress of wondering if you are doing enough.
>
> Schedule your Breaks: This is just as important as scheduling your study time. You will stay motivated and focused if you know that you get to go for a walk, or read something else, or watch a little TV in the near future. Give yourself 10 – 15 minutes of break time for every hour that you study.
>
> Short Term Goals: Set achievable goals each day (or week) for the material you want to cover. This will help you stay focused on a subject or topic. There is a lot to study, and you need to be sure that you are proceeding systematically, so that you don't waste time repeatedly covering the same material.
>
> Actively Read: Don't let yourself skim through subjects. You might as well turn your brain off and stare at the wall, because you will get nothing out of your time. As you read, actively think about what you have read and anticipate what you will read next. If you find yourself passively reading, take your study break and refocus.
>
> Write Things Down: This means using pen and paper. The act of physically transferring ink to paper will help you solidify in your mind what you are studying. Trust us on this. It will take a little more time while you study, but you won't waste time later going back through the same material over and over.

Study Locations: Find a quiet, relaxing place that you can dedicate as a "study zone." Library: good. In front of TV: bad. This location should NOT be your bed, or the couch, or anywhere else you use for sleeping, eating, or relaxing. If you sit at your desk at home, or in the library, you won't be tempted to "watch TV for just a few minutes," or start nodding off because you are in already bed.

Sleep: No surprise here! You need sleep. To prepare yourself, and to help control your nerves when test day comes, get in the habit now of following the same routine each night and going to bed at the same time. Lying awake staring at the ceiling the entire night before the test won't do much good for your score.

Test Day

The Night Before: Take the evening off from studying. Give your mind and body a chance to relax. Eat a healthy dinner with good carbohydrates and get a good night's rest.

Food: On the day of the test, avoid excess coffee and caffeine. Eat a breakfast with lots of fruits, grains, and lean protein to boost your energy and keep you full. Don't substitute sugary candies or sodas for energy.

Think Positively: Seriously! Imagine yourself seeing the questions and thinking confidently, "Hey, I know this answer!"

Be Bold: Don't second-guess questions. Go with your gut instinct, but don't be careless. Make your decision and move forward. Worrying about a question from two pages ago won't help you answer the question you are on now.

Don't Panic: You are prepared. You worked diligently during study time and practice tests and know your own pace. Don't rush, and don't worry about the clock or what anyone else is doing.

Cramming: Do NOT do this! It will only stress you out. And really…come on…do you think you'll actually accomplish something in a couple hours that you couldn't in the weeks you spent studying beforehand?

You SHOULD bring: A watch with which you are familiar and have used during your practice tests, extra batteries for your calculator, a bag or backpack for your belongings, and drinks and snacks for breaks.

What to Leave at Home: Scratch paper, notes and books, cell phones, MP3 players/iPods, highlighters and colored pencils, a timer (like a kitchen timer), or any type of photographic equipment or listening/recording device.

Chapter 1: The English Section

The English portion of the EXPLORE contains five passages, for which you will have two categories of questions: rhetorical, and usage/mechanics. For this section, you will receive three scores: one for each category, and an overall score.

The **usage/mechanics questions** coordinate with numbered, underlined words or phrases. They cover the following concepts:

- **Punctuation:** Apostrophes, colons, semi-colons, commas, dashes, hyphens, quotation marks, parentheses, and their functions in clarifying the meaning of text selections.

- **Basic Grammar:** Verbs, adverbs, adjectives, subject-verb agreement, pronoun-antecedent agreement, and the proper use of connectives.

- **Sentence Structure:** Clauses, modifiers, parallelism, consistency in tense, and point-of-view.

For the **rhetorical questions**, you will be given a passage to read, with questions covering either the entire passage, or separate parts. You will demonstrate your knowledge of:

- **Strategy:** The author's choice of supporting material – if is it effective, applicable, and ample in quality and quantity.

- **Style:** The best choice of adjectives, word order, or alternative wording that most concisely articulates an idea.

- **Organization:** Sentence arrangement within a paragraph, paragraph arrangement within the passage, the need for further information, and the presence of unnecessary information.

English Section Tips

Remember, this is a knowledge-based test, not a reasoning exam. As with all the section tests, you have to know your English grammar. The EXPLORE is not unjustly 'sneaky,' but you do have to be observant and thorough enough to catch errors. Here are some tips to help improve your score.

The Three Main No-No's.
There are three main things the EXPLORE is stringent about:

1. **Redundancy** (repetitious text or words).

2. **Irrelevance** (words or ideas not directly or logically associated with the purpose or main idea).

3. **Wordiness** (drawing out a sentence).

Peruse the entire passage paragraph before answering any of the questions.
Many EXPLORE guides will tell you not to read the entire passage before answering the usage/mechanics questions; however, that approach lends to a greater possibility of error. The overall

meaning or purpose of the paragraph can change the propriety of the highlighted text. For example, looking at just the sentence containing the highlighted word group may cause you to misinterpret the intended parallels or point of view.

Read every word of every question.
Don't assume that you know what is being asked after reading the first few words. Remember, one word at the end of a sentence can change the entire meaning.

Read all the answer choices before making a selection.
Some choices will be partially correct (pertaining to a part, but not all, of the passage) and are intended to catch the eye of the sloppy tester. Note the differences between your answer choices; sometimes they are very subtle.

Understand transitions.
The EXPLORE will require you to recognize the shortest, most proper way to go from one sentence or paragraph to another.

Familiarize yourself with various styles of writing.
The EXPLORE passages may be excerpts from anything: poetry, cause/effect essays, comparison/contrast essays, definition essays, description essays, narration essays, persuasive essays, or process analysis essays.

Learn the directions.
Knowing the directions before test day saves valuable minutes. It enables you to glance quickly at the directions and start answering questions.

> **Standard Directions for the English Section:**
> *In each passage, certain words and phrases have been underlined and numbered. The questions on each passage consist of alternatives for these underlined segments. Choose the alternative that follows standard written English, most accurately reflects the style and tone of the passage, or best relays the idea of the passage. Choose "No Change" if no change is necessary. You are to choose the best answer to the question.*
>
> *You will also find questions about a section of the passage, or the passage as a whole. These questions do not refer to the underlined portions of the passage, but are identified by a boxed number. For each question, choose the alternative that best answers the question.*

Test Your Knowledge: The English Section

Directions:
This test consists of four passages. In each passage, certain words and phrases have been underlined and numbered. The questions on each passage consist of alternatives for these underlined segments. Choose the alternative that follows standard written English, most accurately reflects the style and tone of the passage, or best relays the idea of the passage. Choose "No Change" if no change is necessary.

You are to choose the best answer to the question.

You will also find questions about a section of the passage, or the passage as a whole. These questions do not refer to the underlined portions of the passage, but are identified by a boxed number. For each question, choose the alternative that best answers the question.

PASSAGE I: Examining my Ecological Footprint

Examining the impact my lifestyle has on the earth's resources is <u>a fascinating and valuable thing to do</u>. According to the Earth Day Network ecological footprint calculator created by the Sierra Club, it would take four planet earths to sustain the human population if everyone used as many resources as I do. My "ecological footprint," or the amount of productive area of the earth that is required to produce the resources I consume, <u>must then be much</u> larger

2

<u>like those of</u> most of the population.

3

It is hard to balance the luxuries and opportunities I

1.
   a) NO CHANGE
   b) a fascinating or valuable thing to do.
   c) fascinating to do and also valuable to do.
   d) done to be fascinating or valuable.

2.
   f) NO CHANGE
   g) would have been
   h) much
   j) was much

3.
   a) NO CHANGE
   b) than those of
   c) than footprints of
   d) as the footprints of

have available to me: with doing what I know to be
    4
better from an ecological standpoint.

One's ecological footprint is measured with
                                 5
accounting for different factors such as how often and how far one drives and travels by air, what kind of structure one lives in, and what kind of goods one consumes (and how far those consumer goods travel across the globe). For example, a person who lives in a freestanding home, which uses more energy to heat and cool than an apartment in a building does; who travels internationally several times per year; and who eats exotic, out-of-season foods which must be shipped in from other countries, rather than locally grown and raised food which is in season,
                                     6
would have a large ecological footprint.

   ┌─────┐
   │ 7 │
   └─────┘

4.
   f) NO CHANGE
   g) me, with
   h) me; with
   j) me with

5.
   a) NO CHANGE
   b) measured by
   c) measured with
   d) measured of

6.
   f) NO CHANGE
   g) that are
   h) those are
   j) which are

7. The last sentence in the above paragraph could be improved by:

   a) Being broken into short sentences.
   b) Being moved to the beginning of the paragraph.
   c) Including information about how the footprint is calculated.
   d) Taking out "for example" at the beginning of the sentence.

Although I get points for recycling, my use of public transportation, and living in an apartment complex rather than a free-standing residence; my footprint expands when it is taken into account my not-entirely-local diet, my occasional use of a car, my three magazine subscriptions, and my history of flying more than ten hours a year. These are all examples of things that use a large amount of resources.

[9]

This examination of the impact my lifestyle has on the earth's resources is fascinating and valuable to me. It is fairly easy for me to recycle, so I do it,

8.
 f) NO CHANGE
 g) use of
 h) using
 j) my using

9. The writer wants to add a sentence to the end of the paragraph that encourages others to calculate their own ecological footprint. Which of the following sentences would best accomplish this?

 a) There are many different ways that we use resources that may be surprising.
 b) Other things I do that use high amounts of resources include using a dryer for my laundry and leaving appliances plugged in when I'm out of the house.
 c) Sources of waste are often surprising; you can calculate your own ecological footprint online at myfootprint.org.
 d) Sometimes the best way to reduce one's use of resources is to travel less.

10.
 f) NO CHANGE
 g) on the resources of the planet
 h) had on the earth's resources
 j) has on the earth resources

but it would be much harder to <u>forgoing</u> the
            11
opportunity to travel by plane or eat my favorite

<u>fruits; that</u> have been flown to the supermarket from
       12
a different country. I feel that realizing just how

unfair my share of the <u>earths' resources has</u> been
                              13
should help me to change at least some of my bad

habit. Perhaps if we were all made aware of the true

cost of our habits, actions, and <u>choices, people</u>
                                      14

would be more likely to take steps to reduce <u>his or</u>
                                                 15
<u>her</u> consumption of the earth's resources.

11.
   a) NO CHANGE
   b) forgo
   c) have forgone
   d) not forgo

12.
   f) NO CHANGE
   g) fruits, that
   h) fruits that
   j) fruits: that

13.
   a) NO CHANGE
   b) earth's resources has
   c) earths' resources have
   d) earth's resources have

14.
   f) NO CHANGE
   g) choices. People
   h) choices; people
   j) than people

15.
   a) NO CHANGE
   b) our
   c) their
   d) one's

PASSAGE II
The Sculptor Augusta Savage

Augusta <u>Savage were</u> a world-famous African-
            16

American sculptor. <u>Born in Florida,</u> her first formal
                    17
art training was in New York City at Cooper Union,

the school recommended to her by Solon Gorglum.

<u>While she studied,</u> she supported herself by doing
      18
odd jobs, including clerking and working in

laundries. In 1926 she exhibited her work at the

Sesquicentennial Exposition in Philadelphia. That

same year she was awarded a scholarship to study in

Rome. However, she was unable to accept the

award because she could not raise the money <u>she

would have needed</u> to live there.
        19

When she returned to the United States, she

exhibited her work at several important galleries. <u>In

addition to her own work,</u> Augusta Savage taught
            20
art classes in Harlem. During the Depression, she

helped African- American artists to enroll in the

Works Progress Administration arts project.

16.
   f) NO CHANGE
   g) Savage, was
   h) Savage, were
   j) Savage was

17.
   a) NO CHANGE
   b) She was born in Florida,
   c) While being born inFlorida,
   d) Although she was born in Florida,

18.
   f) NO CHANGE
   g) While she studied
   h) After studying
   j) She studied while

19.
   a) NO CHANGE
   b) she would need
   c) she needed
   d) she needs

20.
   f) NO CHANGE
   g) Additional to creating her own work,
   h) Additionally to her own work,
   j) In addition to creating her own work,

Throughout her career, she was an active spokesperson for African-American artists in the United States. She also was one of the principal
                                                    21
organizers of the Harlem Artists Guild.

In 1923 Savage, applied for a summer art
       22
program sponsored by the French government; despite being more than qualified, she was turned down by the international judging committee, solely because of her race. Savage was deeply upset, questioning the committee, beginning the first of
   23
many public fights for equal rights in her life. The incident got press coverage on both sides of the Atlantic, and eventually the sole supportive committee member, sculptor Hermon Atkins MacNeil—who at one time had shared a studio with Henry Ossawa Tanner—invited her to study with
                                    24
him.

21. The author wants to combine the last two sentences of this paragraph. What is the best way to rewrite the underlined portion?

   a) States; she also
   b) States, although she also
   c) States, and also
   d) States and she

22.
   f) NO CHANGE
   g) 1923 Savage
   h) 1923, Savage
   j) 1923; Savage

23.
   a) NO CHANGE
   b) and questioned
   c) and questioning
   d) and so she questioned

24.
   f) NO CHANGE
   g) invited her to study with himself
   h) invited him to study with her
   j) gave her an invitation to study with him

She later cite him as one of her teachers.
  25

In 1939, Augusta Savage received a commission from the World's Fair and created a 16 foot tall plaster sculpture called *Lift Ev'ry Voice and Sing*. Savage did not have any funds for a bronze cast, or even to move and store it, and it was
  26
destroyed by bulldozers at the close of the fair. However, small metal and plaster souvenir copies of the sculpture has survived.
  27

[28]

Perhaps Savage's more indelible legacy is the work of the students whom she taught in her studio, the Savage Studio of Arts and Crafts. Her students included Jacob Lawrence, Norman Lewis, and Gwendolyn Knight. Lawrence was a Cubist painter whose work is hosted in museums across the country. Lewis was an Abstract Expressionist painter who often dealt with music and jazz in

25.
  a) NO CHANGE
  b) was citing
  c) citing
  d) cited

26.
  f) NO CHANGE
  g) the plaster
  h) them
  j) her

27.
  a) NO CHANGE
  b) have
  c) were
  d) would

28. Which sentence would best fit at the beginning of the paragraph that now begins "In 1939"?

  f) Her education in the arts was substantial after working with so many high profit sculptors.
  g) African-Americans were still facing terrible discrimination at the end of the 1930's.
  h) The World's Fair is a huge art exhibit that occurs every two to four years.
  j) Throughout the 1930's, her profile as an artist continued to grow.

abstract ways. <u>Knight who was born in Barbados</u> founded an organization to support young artists.

29.
a) NO CHANGE
b) Knight, who was born in Barbados
c) Knight who was born in Barbados,
d) Knight, who was born in Barbados,

Augusta Savage <u>worked tireless</u> to teach these artists, help them to secure funding, and support their careers.

30.
f) NO CHANGE
g) worked tirelessly
h) worked herself tireless
j) was working tireless

PASSAGE III
History of Art for Beginners and Students – Ancient Painting

The following passage is adapted from Clara Erskine Clément's History of Art for Beginners and Students, *first published in 1887 (public domain; errors inserted for the purposes of crafting questions).*

In speaking of art we often contrast the useful or mechanical arts with the Fine Arts; by these terms we denote the difference between the arts which are used in making such things as are necessary and useful in civilized life, and the arts by which ornamental and beautiful <u>things made.</u> The fine
              31
arts are Architecture, Sculpture, Painting, Poetry, and Music, and though we could live if none of these <u>existed, yet</u> life would be far from the pleasant
          32
experience that it is often <u>made to be</u> through the
                                    33
enjoyment of these arts.

Of course, forms of art can be both fine and useful. While painting belongs to the fine or beautiful arts, it is a very useful art in many ways. For example, when a school-book is illustrated, how much more easily we understand the subject we are studying through the help we get from pictures of objects or places that we have not otherwise seen.

31.
a) NO CHANGE
b) things.
c) things are made.
d) things are used.

32.
f) NO CHANGE
g) existed,
h) yet,
j) existed and yet

33.
a) NO CHANGE
b) made out to be
c) made
d) is

Pictures of natural scenery bring all countries before our eyes in such a way that by looking at it, while
          34
reading books of travel, we may know a great deal more about lands we have never seen, and may never be able to visit.

[35]

St. Augustine, who wrote in the fourth century,
                                              36
says that "pictures are the books of the simple or unlearned." This is just as true now as then, and we should regard pictures as one of the best methods for teaching. The cultivation of the imagination is very important because for this way
                              37
we can add much to our individual happiness. Thus one of the uses of pictures is that they give us a clear idea of what we have not seen; a second use is

34.
   f) NO CHANGE
   g) those
   h) them
   j) one

35. Which of the following sentences could be added to the above paragraph to give another example of how pictures are useful as well as decorative?

   a) Pictures are not useful, however, when they distract students from the purpose of a text.
   b) Pictures can be a beautiful addition to our homes.
   c) Doctors often use pictures when studying the body to help them learn organs and systems.
   d) This is helpful because people really don't travel to other lands anymore.

36.
   f) NO CHANGE
   g) century says
   h) century said
   j) century, said

37.
   a) NO CHANGE
   b) important, because in
   c) important, because for
   d) important; in

that they are exciting to our imaginations, and often
                    38
help us to forget disagreeable circumstances and unpleasant surroundings. Through this power, if we are in a dark, narrow street, in a house which is not to our liking, or in the midst of any unpleasant
                              39
happenings, we are able to fix our thoughts upon a photograph or picture that may be there, and we are able to imagine ourselves far, far away, in some spot where nature makes everything pleasant and soothes us into forgetfulness of all that makes us unhappy. Many an invalid—many an unfortunate person is made content by pictures during hours that would otherwise be wretched.
                                          40

This is the result of cultivating the imagination and when this is done, we have a source of pleasure
  41
within ourselves which can never be taken from us.

It often happens that we see two people doing
                                            42
the same work and are situated in the same way in

38.
f) NO CHANGE
g) exciting
h) excite
j) excited

39. If the writer deletes this section of this sentence, what will be lost?

a) Nothing; the meaning of the sentence will not change.
b) The argument that pictures are useful.
c) The example of pictures being educational.
d) The generalization of the specific example to all unpleasant circumstances.

40.
f) NO CHANGE
g) tend to be
h) however be
j) be

41.
a) NO CHANGE
b) imagination so when
c) imagination, and when
d) imagination; when

42.
f) NO CHANGE
g) are doing
h) who do
j) done

the world, but who are different in their <u>manner</u>
                                              43
<u>one</u> is light-hearted and happy, the other sullen and

sad. If you can find out the truth, it will be that

the sad one is matter-of-fact, and has no

imagination—he can only think of his work and

what concerns him personally; but the merry one

would surprise you if you could read his thoughts—

if you could know the distances <u>they have</u> passed
                                         44

over, and what a vast difference there is between his

thought and his work. So while it is natural for

almost everyone to exclaim <u>joyful</u> at the beauty of
                                    45
pictures, and to enjoy looking at them simply, I

wish my readers to think of their uses also, and

understand the benefits that may be derived from

them.

43.
   a) NO CHANGE
   b) manner; one
   c) manner. One
   d) manner: one

44.
   f) NO CHANGE
   g) he has
   h) it has
   j) you have

45.
   a) NO CHANGE
   b) joyfully
   c) joy
   d) with joy

Test Your Knowledge: The English Section – Answers

1. a)
2. f)
3. b)
4. j)
5. b)
6. f)
7. a)
8. h) This is an instance of parallelism, where you want verbs in a list in a sentence to have the same form.
9. c)
10. f)
11. b)
12. h)
13. b)
14. f)
15. c)
16. j)
17. d) This is an example of a misplaced modifier and needs to be edited.
18. f)
19. a)
20. j)
21. c)
22. h)
23. b)
24. f)
25. d)
26. g)
27. b)
28. j) This sentence best follows the topic of the passage while leading into the new information in this paragraph.
29. d)
30. g)
31. c)
32. g)
33. d)
34. h)
35. c)
36. f)
37. b)
38. h)
39. d)
40. f)
41. c)
42. h)
43. d)
44. f)
45. b)

Chapter 2: The Math Section

Before we begin our review, remember that there is no wrong-answer penalty on this exam, so try not to leave an answer selection blank. Of course, since the objective is to get as many right answers as possible, always use the process of elimination before choosing your answer. While the amount of time allotted for this section may seem like too little for the amount of questions, many of the questions are designed to be simpler than others. We recommend going through the exam first, quickly answering those questions which seem easier than others. Then, on your second run-through, focus your attention on the more-complicated problems.

The Most Common Mistakes

People make mistakes all the time – but during a test, those mistakes can cost you a passing score. Watch out for these common mistakes that people make on the EXPLORE:

- Answering with the wrong sign (positive / negative).

- Mixing up the Order of Operations.

- Misplacing a decimal.

- Not reading the question thoroughly (and therefore providing an answer that was not asked for.)

- Circling the wrong letter, or filling in wrong circle choice.

If you're thinking, "Those ideas are just common sense" – exactly! Most of the mistakes made on the EXPLORE are simple mistakes. Regardless, they still result in a wrong answer and the loss of a potential point.

Helpful Strategies

1. **Go Back to the Basics**: First and foremost, practice your basic skills: sign changes, order of operations, simplifying fractions, and equation manipulation. These are the skills used most on the test, though they are applied in different contexts. Remember that when it comes right down to it, all math problems rely on the four basic skills of addition, subtraction, multiplication, and division. All that changes is the order in which they are used to solve a problem.

2. **Don't Rely on Mental Math**: Using mental math is great for eliminating answer choices, but ALWAYS WRITE IT DOWN! This cannot be stressed enough. Use whatever paper is provided; by writing and/or drawing out the problem, you are more likely to catch any mistakes. The act of writing things down forces you to organize your calculations, leading to an improvement in your score.

3. **The Three-Times Rule**:

    - **Step One – Read the question**: Write out the given information.

    - **Step Two – Read the question**: Set up your equation(s) and solve.

    - **Step Three – Read the question:** Make sure that your answer makes sense (is the amount too large or small, is the answer in the correct unit of measure, etc.).

4. **Make an Educated Guess**: Eliminate those answer choices which you are relatively sure are incorrect, and then guess from the remaining choices. Educated guessing is critical to increasing your score.

Calculators

Calculators may only be used on the mathematics section, but all the questions can be answered without one. You may use any four-function, scientific, or graphing calculator, unless it has the following features which are prohibited.

As stated before, you may **NOT** use a calculator with the following functions:

- Calculators with built-in computer algebra systems.

- Texas Instruments: TI – 89, TI – 92.

- Hewlett-Packard: hp 48GII, and all models beginning with hp 40G, hp 49G, or hp50G.

- Casio: Algebra fx 2.0, ClassPad 300, and all models beginning with CFX-9970G.

- Pocket organizers.

- Handheld or laptop computers.

- Electronic writing pads or pen-input devices.

- Calculators with a typewriter keypad (QWERTY).

- Calculators built into cell phones or other electronic devices.

Math Concepts Tested on the EXPLORE

You need to practice in order to score well on the test. To make the most out of your practice, use this guide to determine the areas for which you need more review. Most importantly, practice all areas under testing circumstances (a quiet area, a timed practice test, no looking up facts as you practice, etc.)

When reviewing, take your time and let your brain recall the necessary math. If you are taking this test, then you have already had course instruction in these areas. The examples given will "jog" your memory.

The next few pages will cover various math subjects (starting with the basics, but in no particular order), along with worked examples.

Order of Operations

PEMDAS – Parentheses/Exponents/Multiply/Divide/Add/Subtract

Perform the operations within parentheses first, and then any exponents. After those steps, perform all multiplication and division. (These are done from left to right, as they appear in the problem) Finally, do all required addition and subtraction, also from left to right as they appear in the problem.

Examples:

Solve $(-(2)^2 - (4 + 7))$.

$(-4 - 11) = -\mathbf{15}$.

Solve $((5)^2 \div 5 + 4 * 2)$.

$25 \div 5 + 4 * 2$.

$5 + 8 = \mathbf{13}$.

Positive & Negative Number Rules

$(+) + (-)$ = Subtract the two numbers. Solution gets the sign of the larger number.

$(-) + (-)$ = Negative number.

$(-) * (-)$ = Positive number.

$(-) * (+)$ = Negative number.

$(-) / (-)$ = Positive number.

$(-) / (+)$ = Negative number.

Fractions

Adding and subtracting fractions requires a common denominator.

Find a common denominator for:

$$\frac{2}{3} - \frac{1}{5}$$

$$\frac{2}{3} - \frac{1}{5} = \frac{2}{3}\left(\frac{5}{5}\right) - \frac{1}{5}\left(\frac{3}{3}\right) = \frac{10}{15} - \frac{3}{15} = \frac{7}{15}$$

To add mixed fractions, work first the whole numbers, and then the fractions.

$$2\frac{1}{4} + 1\frac{3}{4} = 3\frac{4}{4} = \mathbf{4}$$

To subtract mixed fractions, convert to single fractions by multiplying the whole number by the denominator and adding the numerator. Then work as above.

$$2\frac{1}{4} - 1\frac{3}{4} = \frac{9}{4} - \frac{7}{4} = \frac{2}{4} = \frac{1}{2}$$

To multiply fractions, convert any mixed fractions into single fractions and multiply across; reduce to lowest terms if needed.

$$2\frac{1}{4} * 1\frac{3}{4} = \frac{9}{4} * \frac{7}{4} = \frac{63}{16} = 3\frac{15}{16}$$

To divide fractions, convert any mixed fractions into single fractions, flip the second fraction, and then multiply across.

$$2\frac{1}{4} \div 1\frac{3}{4} = \frac{9}{4} \div \frac{7}{4} = \frac{9}{4} * \frac{4}{7} = \frac{36}{28} = 1\frac{8}{28} = 1\frac{2}{7}$$

Absolute Value

The absolute value of a number is its distance from zero, not its value.

So in $|x| = a$, "x" will equal "-a" as well as "a."

Likewise, $|3| = 3$, and $|-3| = 3$.

Equations with absolute values will have two answers. Solve each absolute value possibility separately. All solutions must be checked into the original equation.

Example: Solve for x:
$|2x - 3| = x + 1$.

Equation One: $2x - 3 = -(x + 1)$.
$2x - 3 = -x - 1$.
$3x = 2$.
x = 2/3.

Equation Two: $2x - 3 = x + 1$.
x = 4.

Simple Interest

Interest * Principle

Example: If I deposit $500 into an account with an annual rate of 5%, how much will I have after 2 years?

1st year: $500 + (500*.05) = 525$.

2nd year: $525 + (525*.05) = \mathbf{551.25}$.

Greatest Common Factor (GCF)

The greatest factor that divides two numbers.

Example: The GCF of 24 and 18 is 6. 6 is the largest number, or greatest factor, that can divide both 24 and 18.

Mean, Median, Mode

Mean is a math term for "average." Total all terms and divide by the number of terms.

Find the mean of 24, 27, and 18.

24 + 27 + 18 = 69 ÷ 3 = **23**.

Median is the middle number of a given set, found after the numbers have all been put in numerical order. In the case of a set of even numbers, the middle two numbers are averaged.

What is the median of 24, 27, and 18?

18, **24**, 27.

What is the median of 24, 27, 18, and 19?

18, 19, 24, 27 (19 + 24 = 43. 43/2 = **21.5**).

Mode is the number which occurs most frequently within a given set.

What is the mode of 2, 5, 4, 4, 3, 2, 8, 9, 2, 7, 2, and 2?

The mode would be **2** because it appears the most within the set.

Percent, Part, & Whole

Part = Percent * Whole.

Percent = Part / Whole.

Whole = Part / Percent.

Example: Jim spent 30% of his paycheck at the fair. He spent $15 for a hat, $30 for a shirt, and $20 playing games. How much was his check? (Round to nearest dollar)

Whole = 65 / .30 = **$217.00**.

Percent Change

Percent Change = Amount of Change / Original Amount * 100.

Percent Increase = (New Amount − Original Amount) / Original Amount * 100.

Percent Decrease = (Original Amount − New Amount) / Original Amount * 100.

Amount Increase (or **Decrease**) = Original Price * Percent Markup (or Markdown).

Original Price = New Price / (Whole − Percent Markdown).

Original Price = New Price / (Whole + Percent Markup).

> **Example:** A car that was originally priced at $8300 has been reduced to $6995. What percent has it been reduced?
>
> (8300 − 6995) / 8300 * 100 = **15.72%**.

Repeated Percent Change

Increase: Final amount = Original Amount * $(1 + \text{Rate})^{\text{\# of changes}}$.

Decrease: Final Amount = Original Amount * $(1 - \text{Rate})^{\text{\# of changes}}$.

> **Example:** The weight of a tube of toothpaste decreases by 3% each time it is used. If it weighed 76.5 grams when new, what is its weight in grams after 15 uses?
>
> Final amount = $76.5 * (1 - .3)^{15}$.
>
> $76.5 * (.97)^{15}$ = **48.44 grams**.

Ratios

To solve a ratio, simply find the equivalent fraction. To distribute a whole across a ratio:

1. Total all parts.

2. Divide the whole by the total number of parts.

3. Multiply quotient by corresponding part of ratio.

> **Example:** There are 90 voters in a room, and they are either Democrat or Republican. The ratio of Democrats to Republicans is 5:4. How many Republicans are there?
>
> Step 1   5 + 4 = 9.
>
> Step 2   90 / 9 = 10.
>
> Step 3   10 * 4 = **40 Republicans**.

Proportions

Direct Proportions: Corresponding ratio parts change in the same direction (increase/decrease).

Indirect Proportions: Corresponding ratio parts change in opposite directions (as one part increases the other decreases).

Example: A train traveling 120 miles takes 3 hours to get to its destination. How long will it take if the train travels 180 miles?

120 mph:180 mph is to x hours:3 hours.

(Write as fraction and cross multiply.)

120/3 = 180/x.

540 = 120x.

x = **4.5 hours.**

Probabilities

A probability is found by dividing the number of desired outcomes by the number of possible outcomes. (The piece divided by the whole.)

Example: What is the probability of picking a blue marble if 3 of the 15 marbles are blue?

3/15 = 1/5. The probability is **1 in 5** that a blue marble is picked.

Math and Quantitative Reasoning Sequence

Each term is equal to the previous term plus x.

Example: 2, 5, 8, 11.

x = **3**.

2 + 3 = 5; 5 + 3 = 8 ... etc.

Geometric Sequence

Each term is equal to the previous term multiplied by x.

Example: 2, 4, 8, 16.

x = **2**.

Prime Factorization

Expand to prime number factors.

Example: $104 = 2 * 2 * 2 * 13$.

Exponent Rules

Rule	Example
$x^0 = 1$	$5^0 = 1$
$x^1 = x$	$5^1 = 5$
$x^a \cdot x^b = x^{a+b}$	$5^2 * 5^3 = 5^5$
$(xy)^a = x^a y^a$	$(5*6)^2 = 5^2 * 6^2 = 25 * 36$
$(x^a)^b = x^{ab}$	$(5^2)^3 = 5^6$
$(x/y)^a = x^a/y^a$	$(10/5)^2 = 10^2/5^2 = 100/25$
$x^a/y^b = x^{a-b}$	$5^4/5^3 = 5^1 = 5$ (remember $x \neq 0$)
$x^{1/a} = \sqrt[a]{x}$	$25^{1/2} = \sqrt[2]{25} = 5$
$x^{-a} = \frac{1}{x^a}$	$5^{-2} = \frac{1}{5^2} = \frac{1}{25}$ (remember $x \neq 0$)
$(-x)^a$ = positive number if "a" is even; negative number if "a" is odd.	

Roots

Root of a Product: $\sqrt[n]{a \cdot b} = \sqrt[n]{a} \cdot \sqrt[n]{b}$

Root of a Quotient: $\sqrt[n]{\frac{a}{b}} = \frac{\sqrt[n]{a}}{\sqrt[n]{b}}$

Fractional Exponent: $\sqrt[n]{a^m} = a^{m/n}$

Literal Equations

Equations with more than one variable. Solve in terms of one variable first.

Example: Solve for y: $4x + 3y = 3x + 2y$.

Step 1 – Combine like terms: $3y - 2y = 4x - 2x$.

Step 2 – Solve for y: $y = 2x$.

Slope

The formula used to calculate the slope (*m*) of a straight line connecting two points is: $m = (y_2 - y_1) / (x_2 - x_1)$ = change in *y* / change in *x*.

Example: Calculate slope of the line in the diagram:

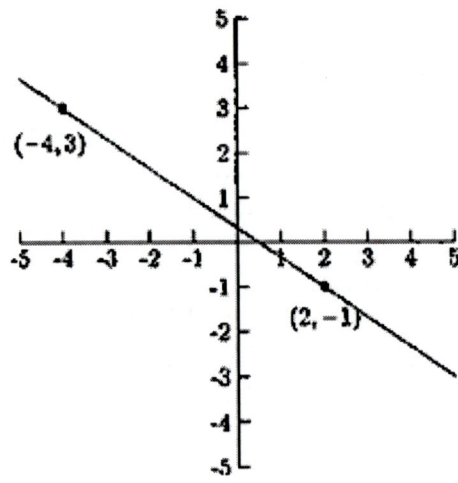

$m = (3 - (-1))/(-4 - 2) = 4/-6 = -2/3$.

Midpoint

To determine the midpoint between two points, simply add the two *x* coordinates together and divide by 2 (midpoint *x*). Then add the *y* coordinates together and divide by 2 (midpoint *y*).

$$\left(\frac{x_1 + x_2}{2}, \frac{y_1 + y}{2}\right)$$

Algebraic Equations

When simplifying or solving algebraic equations, you need to be able to utilize all math rules: exponents, roots, negatives, order of operations, etc.

1. Add & Subtract: Only the coefficients of like terms.

    Example: $5xy + 7y + 2yz + 11xy - 5yz = 16xy + 7y - 3yz$.

2. Multiplication: First the coefficients then the variables.

    Example: Monomial * Monomial.

    $(3x^4y^2z)(2y^4z^5) = 6x^4y^6z^6$.

    (A variable with no exponent has an implied exponent of 1.)

    Example: Monomial * Polynomial.

    $(2y^2)(y^3 + 2xy^2z + 4z) = 2y^5 + 4xy^4z + 8y^2z$.

Example: Binomial * Binomial.

$(5x + 2)(3x + 3)$.

(Remember FOIL – First, Outer, Inner, Last.)

First: $5x * 3x = 15x^2$.

Outer: $5x * 3 = 15x$.

Inner: $2 * 3x = 6x$.

Last: $2 * 3 = 6$.

Combine like terms: $15x^2 + 21x + 6$.

Example: Binomial * Polynomial.

$(x + 3)(2x^2 - 5x - 2)$.

First term: $x(2x^2 - 5x - 2) = 2x^3 - 5x^2 - 2x$.

Second term: $3(2x^2 - 5x - 2) = 6x^2 - 15x - 6$.

Added Together: $2x^3 + x^2 - 17x - 6$.

Inequalities

Inequalities are solved like linear and algebraic equations, except the sign must be reversed when dividing by a negative number.

Example: $-7x + 2 < 6 - 5x$.

Step 1 – Combine like terms: $-2x < 4$.

Step 2 – Solve for x. (Reverse the sign): **$x > -2$.**

Solving compound inequalities will give you two answers.

Example: $-4 \leq 2x - 2 \leq 6$.

Step 1 – Add 2 to each term to isolate x: $-2 \leq 2x \leq 8$.

Step 2: Divide by 2: $-1 \leq x \leq 4$.

Solution set is **[-1, 4]**.

Fundamental Counting Principle

(The number of possibilities of an event happening) * (the number of possibilities of another event happening) = the total number of possibilities.

Example: If you take a multiple choice test with 5 questions, with 4 answer choices for each question, how many test result possibilities are there?

Solution: Question 1 has 4 choices; question 2 has 4 choices; etc.

4 *4 * 4 * 4 * 4 (one for each question) = **1024 possible test results**.

Permutations

The number of ways a set number of items can be arranged. Recognized by the use of a factorial (n!), with n being the number of items.

If n = 3, then 3! = 3 * 2 * 1 = 6. If you need to arrange n number of things but *x* number are alike, then n! is divided by *x*!

Example: How many different ways can the letters in the word **balance** be arranged?

Solution: There are 7 letters so *n!* = *7!* and 2 letters are the same so *x!* = *2!* Set up the equation:

$$\frac{7*6*5*4*3*2*1}{2*1} = \textbf{2540 ways.}$$

Combinations

To calculate total number of possible combinations use the formula:
n!/r! (n-r)!   n = # of objects   r = # of objects selected at a time

Example: If seven people are selected in groups of three, how many different combinations are possible?

Solution:
$$\frac{7*6*5*4*3*2*1}{(3*2*1)(7-3)} = \textbf{210 possible combinations.}$$

Geometry

- **Acute Angle**: Measures less than 90°.

- **Acute Triangle**: Each angle measures less than 90°.

- **Obtuse Angle**: Measures greater than 90°.

- **Obtuse Triangle**: One angle measures greater than 90°.

- **Adjacent Angles**: Share a side and a vertex.

- **Complementary Angles**: Adjacent angles that sum to 90°.

- **Supplementary Angles**: Adjacent angles that sum to 180°.

- **Vertical Angles**: Angles that are opposite of each other. They are always congruent (equal in measure).

- **Equilateral Triangle**: All angles are equal.

- **Isosceles Triangle**: Two sides and two angles are equal.

- **Scalene**: No equal angles.

- **Parallel Lines**: Lines that will never intersect. Y ‖ X means line Y is parallel to line X.

- **Perpendicular lines**: Lines that intersect or cross to form 90° angles.

- **Transversal Line**: A line that crosses parallel lines.

- **Bisector**: Any line that cuts a line segment, angle, or polygon exactly in half.

- **Polygon**: Any enclosed plane shape with three or more connecting sides (ex. a triangle).

- **Regular Polygon**: Has all equal sides and equal angles (ex. square).

- **Arc**: A portion of a circle's edge.

- **Chord**: A line segment that connects two different points on a circle.

- **Tangent**: Something that touches a circle at only one point without crossing through it.

- **Sum of Angles**: The sum of angles of a polygon can be calculated using $(n-1)180°$, when n = the number of sides

Know the Names of Sided Plane Figures:

Number of Sides	Name
3	Triangle (or Trigon)
4	Quadrilateral (or Tetragon)
5	Pentagon
6	Hexagon
7	Heptagon
8	Octagon
9	Nonagon

Number of Sides	Name
11	Hendecagon
12	Dodecagon
13	Tridecagon
14	Tetradecagon
15	Pentadecagon
16	Hexadecagon
17	Heptadecagon
18	Octadecagon
10	Decagon

Regular Polygons

Polygon Angle Principle: S = The sum of interior angles of a polygon with n-sides.

$S = (n - 2)180$.

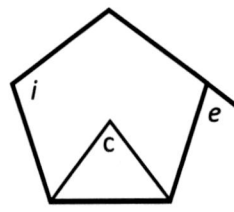

The measure of each central angle (c) is $360°/n$.
The measure of each interior angle (i) is $(n - 2)180°/n$.
The measure of each exterior angle (e) is $360°/n$.

To compare areas of similar polygons: $A_1/A_2 = (side_1/side_2)^2$.

Triangles

The angles in a triangle add up to $180°$.

Area of a triangle = ½ * b * h, or ½bh.

Pythagoras' Theorem: $a^2 + b^2 = c^2$.

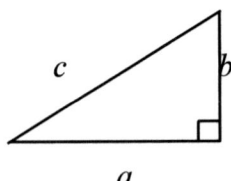

Trapezoids

Four-sided polygon, in which the bases (and only the bases) are parallel.
Isosceles Trapezoid – base angles are congruent.

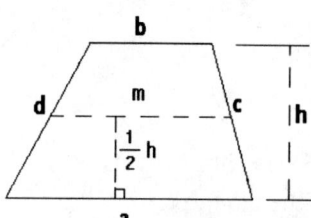

Area and Perimeter of a Trapezoid

$$m = \frac{1}{2}(a + b)$$

$$Area = \frac{1}{2}h * (a + b) = m * h$$

$$Perimeter = a + b + c + d = 2m + c + d$$

If m is the median then: $m \parallel \overline{AB}$ and $m \parallel CD$

Rhombus

Four-sided polygon, in which all four sides are congruent and opposite sides are parallel.

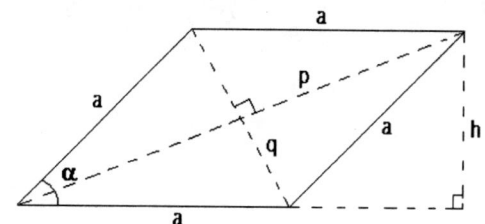

Area and Perimeter of a Rhombus

$$Perimeter = 4a$$

$$Area = a^2 \sin\alpha = a * h = \frac{1}{2}pq$$

$$4a^2 = p^2 + q^2$$

Rectangle

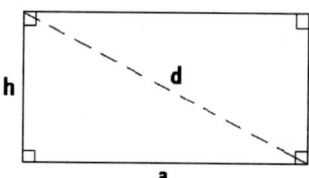

Area and Perimeter of a Rectangle

$$d = \sqrt{a^2 + h^2}$$

$$a = \sqrt{d^2 - h^2}$$

$$h = \sqrt{d^2 - a^2}$$

$$Perimeter = 2a + 2h$$

$$Area = a \cdot h$$

Square

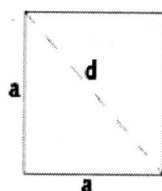

Area and Perimeter of a Square

$$d = a\sqrt{2}$$

$$Perimeter = 4a = 2d\sqrt{2}$$

$$Area = a^2 = \frac{1}{2}d^2$$

Circle

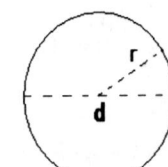

Area and Perimeter of a Circle

$d = 2r$

$Perimeter = 2\pi r = \pi d$

$Area = \pi r^2$

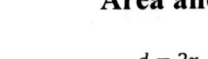

The product length of one chord equals the product length of the other, or:

AB=CD

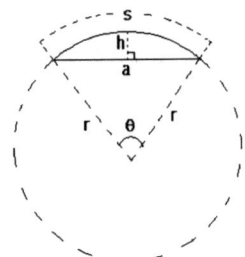

Area and Perimeter of the Sector of a Circle

$\alpha = \dfrac{\theta \pi}{180}$ (rad)

$s = r\alpha$

$Perimeter = 2r + s$

$Area = \dfrac{1}{2} \theta\, r^2$ $(radians)$ or $\dfrac{n}{360}\pi r^2$

length (l) of an arc $l = \dfrac{\pi n r}{180}$ or $\dfrac{n}{360} 2\pi r$

Area and Perimeter of the Segment of a Circle

$\alpha = \dfrac{\theta \pi}{180}$ (rad)

$a = 2\sqrt{2hr - h^2}$

$a^2 = 2r^2 - 2r^2 \cos\theta$

$s = r\alpha$

$h = r - \dfrac{1}{2}\sqrt{4r^2 - a^2}$

$Perimeter = a + s$

$Area = \dfrac{1}{2}[sr - a(r - h)]$

Cube

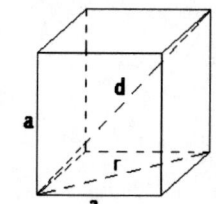

Area and Volume of a Cube

$r = a\sqrt{2}$

$d = a\sqrt{3}$

$Area = 6a^2$

$Volume = a^3$

Cuboid

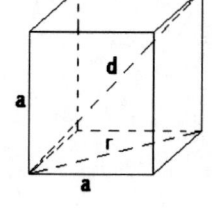

Area and Volume of a Cuboid

$d = \sqrt{a^2 + b^2 + c^2}$

$A = 2(ab + ac + bc)$

$V = abc$

Pyramid

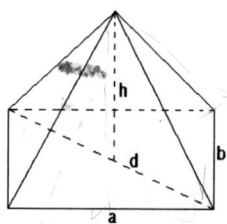

Area and Volume of a Pyramid

$A_{lateral} = a\sqrt{h^2 + \left(\frac{b}{2}\right)^2} + b\sqrt{h^2 + \left(\frac{a}{2}\right)^2}$

$d = \sqrt{a^2 + b^2}$

$A_{base} = ab$

$A_{total} = A_{lateral} + A_{base}$

$V = \frac{1}{3}abh$

Cylinder

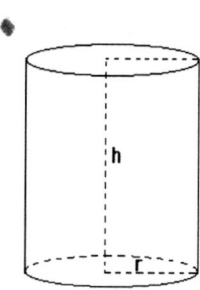

Area and Volume of a Cylinder

$d = 2r$

$A_{surface} = 2\pi rh$

$A_{base} = 2\pi r^2$

$Area = A_{surface} + A_{base}$

$ = 2\pi r(h + r)$

$Volume = \pi r^2 h$

Cone

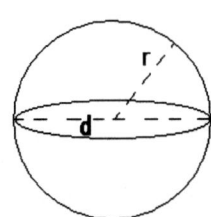

Area and Volume of a Cone

$d = 2r$

$A_{surface} = \pi rs$

$A_{base} = \pi r^2$

$Area = A_{surface} + A_{base}$

$ = 2\pi r(h + r)$

$Volume = \frac{1}{3}\pi r^2 h$

Sphere

Area and Volume of a Sphere

$d = 2r$

$A_{surface} = 4\pi r^2$

$Volume = \frac{4}{3}\pi r^3$

Test Your Knowledge: The Math Section

1. $3 * (2 * 4^3) \div 4 = ?$

2. $(4^3 + 2 - 1) = ?$

3. $(5 * 3) * 1 + 5 = ?$

4. $(7^2 - 2^3 - 6) = ?$

5. $(5^3 + 7) * 2 = ?$

6. If Lynn can type a page in p minutes, how many pages can she do in 5 minutes?
    a) $5/p$.
    b) $p - 5$.
    c) $p + 5$.
    d) $p/5$.
    e) $1 - p + 5$.

7. If Sally can paint a house in 4 hours, and John can paint the same house in 6 hours, how long will it take for both of them to paint the house together?
    a) 2 hours and 24 minutes.
    b) 3 hours and 12 minutes.
    c) 3 hours and 44 minutes.
    d) 4 hours and 10 minutes.
    e) 4 hours and 33 minutes.

8. The sales price of a car is $12,590, which is 20% off the original price. What is the original price?
    a) $14,310.40.
    b) $14,990.90.
    c) $15,290.70.
    d) $15,737.50.
    e) $16,935.80.

9. Solve the following equation for "A": $2A \div 3 = 8 + 4A$.
    a) -2.4.
    b) 2.4.
    c) 1.3.
    d) -1.3.
    e) 0.

10. If $y = 3$, then what is $y^3(y^3 - y)$?
    a) 300.
    b) 459.
    c) 648.
    d) 999.
    e) 1099.

11. Round 907.457 to the nearest tens place.
    a) 908.0.
    b) 910.
    c) 907.5.
    d) 900.
    e) 907.46

12. What is 1230.932567 rounded to the nearest hundredths place?
    a) 1200.
    b) 1230.9326.
    c) 1230.93.
    d) 1230.
    e) 1230.933.

13. Subtract the following numbers (First minus second minus third), and round to the nearest tenths place:

    134.679
    45.548
    67.8807

    a) 21.3.
    b) 21.25.
    c) –58.97.
    d) –59.0.
    e) 1.

14. What is the absolute value of –9?
    a) –9.
    b) 9.
    c) 0.
    d) –1.
    e) 1.

15. What is the median of the following list of numbers: 4, 5, 7, 9, 10, and 12?
    a) 6.
    b) 7.5.
    c) 7.8.
    d) 8.
    e) 9.

16. What is the mathematical average of the number of weeks in a year, seasons in a year, and the number of days in January?
    a) 36.
    b) 33.
    c) 32.
    d) 31.
    e) 29.

17. 0.98 + 45.102 + 32.3333 + 31 + 0.00009 = ?
   a) 368.573.
   b) 210.536299.
   c) 109.41539.
   d) 99.9975.
   e) 80.8769543.

18. Find 0.12 ÷ 1.
   a) 12.
   b) 1.2.
   c) .12.
   d) .012.
   e) .0012.

19. (9 ÷ 3) * (8 ÷ 4) = ?
   a) 1.
   b) 6.
   c) 72.
   d) 576.
   e) 752.

20. 6 * 0 * 5 = ?
   a) 30.
   b) 11.
   c) 25.
   d) 0.
   e) 27.

21. 7.95 ÷ 1.5 = ?
   a) 2.4
   b) 5.3
   c) 6.2
   d) 7.3
   e) 7.5

22. Describe the following sequence in mathematical terms: 144, 72, 36, 18, and 9.
   a) Descending arithmetic sequence.
   b) Ascending arithmetic sequence.
   c) Descending geometric sequence.
   d) Ascending geometric sequence.
   e) Miscellaneous sequence.

23. Which of the following is not a whole number followed by its square?
   a) 1, 1.
   b) 6, 36.
   c) 8, 64.
   d) 10, 100.
   e) 11, 144.

24. There are 12 more apples than oranges in a basket of 36 apples and oranges. How many apples are in the basket?
    a) 12.
    b) 15.
    c) 24.
    d) 28.
    e) 36.

25. Which of the following correctly identifies 4 consecutive odd integers, where the sum of the middle two integers is equal to 24?
    a) 5, 7, 9, 11.
    b) 7, 9, 11, 13.
    c) 9, 11, 13, 15.
    d) 11, 13, 15, 17.
    e) 13, 15, 17, 19.

26. What is the next number in the sequence? 6, 12, 24, 48, ___.
    a) 72.
    b) 96.
    c) 108.
    d) 112.
    e) 124.

27. If the perimeter of a rectangular house is 44 yards, and the length is 36 feet, what is the width of the house?
    a) 30 feet.
    b) 18 yards.
    c) 28 feet.
    d) 32 feet.
    e) 36 yards.

28. What is the volume of a cylinder with a diameter of 1 foot and a height of 14 inches?
    a) 2104.91 cubic inches.
    b) 1584 cubic inches.
    c) 528 cubic inches.
    d) 904.32 cubic inches.
    e) 264 cubic inches.

29. What is the volume of a cube whose width is 5 inches?
    a) 15 cubic inches.
    b) 25 cubic inches.
    c) 64 cubic inches.
    d) 100 cubic inches.
    e) 125 cubic inches.

30. A can's diameter is 3 inches, and its height is 8 inches. What is the volume of the can?
    a) 50.30 cubic inches.
    b) 56.57 cubic inches.
    c) 75.68 cubic inches.
    d) 113.04 cubic inches.
    e) 226.08 cubic inches.

31. If the area of a square flowerbed is 16 square feet, then how many feet is the perimeter of the flowerbed?
    a) 4.
    b) 12.
    c) 16.
    d) 20.
    e) 24.

32. If a discount of 25% off the retail price of a desk saves Mark $45, what was the original price of the desk?
    a) $135.
    b) $160.
    c) $180.
    d) $210.
    e) $215.

33. A customer pays $1,100 in state taxes on a newly-purchased car. What is the value of the car if state taxes are 8.9% of the value?
    a) $9.765.45
    b) $10,876.90
    c) $12,359.55
    d) $14,345.48
    e) $15,745.45

34. 35% of what number is 70?
    a) 100.
    b) 110.
    c) 150.
    d) 175.
    e) 200.

35. What number is 5% of 2000?
    a) 50.
    b) 100.
    c) 150.
    d) 200.
    e) 250.

Test Your Knowledge: The Math Section – Answers

1. 96.
2. 65.
3. 20.
4. 35.
5. 264.
6. a)
7. a)
8. d)
9. a)
10. c)
11. b)
12. c)
13. a)
14. b)
15. d)
16. e)
17. c)
18. c)
19. b)
20. d)
21. b)
22. c)
23. e)
24. c)
25. c)
26. b)
27. a)
28. b)
29. e)
30. b)
31. c)
32. c)
33. c)
34. e)
35. b)

Chapter 3: The Reading Section

The Reading section of the EXPLORE measures your ability to understand, analyze, and evaluate written passages. The passages will contain material from a variety of sources, and will cover a number of different topics.

There are many elements within the passages which you will be asked to identify and/or comprehend.

The Main Idea

Finding and understanding the main idea of a text is an essential reading skill. When you look past the facts and information and get to the heart of what the writer is trying to say, that's the **main idea**.

Imagine that you're at a friend's home for the evening:

> "Here," he says, "Let's watch this movie."

> "Sure," you reply. "What's it about?"

You'd like to know a little about what you'll be watching, but your question may not get you a satisfactory answer, because you've only asked about the subject of the film. The subject—what the movie is about—is only half the story. Think, for example, about all the alien invasion films ever been made. While these films may share the same general subject, what they have to say about the aliens or about humanity's theoretical response to invasion may be very different. Each film has different ideas it wants to convey about a subject, just as writers write because they have something they want to say about a particular subject. When you look beyond the facts and information to what the writer really wants to say about his or her subject, you're looking for the main idea.

One of the most common questions on reading comprehension exams is, "What is the main idea of this passage?" How would you answer this question for the paragraph below?

> "Wilma Rudolph, the crippled child who became an Olympic running champion, is an inspiration for us all. Born prematurely in 1940, Wilma spent her childhood battling illness, including measles, scarlet fever, chicken pox, pneumonia, and polio, a crippling disease which at that time had no cure. At the age of four, she was told she would never walk again. But Wilma and her family refused to give up. After years of special treatment and physical therapy, 12-year-old Wilma was able to walk normally again. But walking wasn't enough for Wilma, who was determined to be an athlete. Before long, her talent earned her a spot in the 1956 Olympics, where she earned a bronze medal. In the 1960 Olympics, the height of her career, she won three gold medals."

What is the main idea of this paragraph? You might be tempted to answer, "Wilma Rudolph" or "Wilma Rudolph's life." Yes, Wilma Rudolph's life is the **subject** of the passage—who or what the passage is about—but the subject is not necessarily the main idea. The **main idea** is what the writer wants to say about this subject. What is the main thing the writer says about Wilma's life?

Which of the following statements is the main idea of the paragraph?

    a) Wilma Rudolph was very sick as a child.
    b) Wilma Rudolph was an Olympic champion.
    c) Wilma Rudolph is someone to admire.

Main idea: The overall fact, feeling, or thought a writer wants to convey about his or her subject.

The best answer is **c)**: Wilma Rudolph is someone to admire. This is the idea the paragraph adds up to; it's what holds all of the information in the paragraph together. This example also shows two important characteristics of a main idea:

1. It is **general** enough to encompass all of the ideas in the passage.

2. It is an **assertion.** An assertion is a statement made by the writer.

The main idea of a passage must be general enough to encompass all of the ideas in the passage. It should be broad enough for all of the other sentences in that passage to fit underneath it, like people under an umbrella. Notice that the first two options, "Wilma Rudolph was very sick as a child" and "Wilma Rudolph was an Olympic champion", are too specific to be the main idea. They aren't broad enough to cover all of the ideas in the passage, because the passage talks about both her illnesses and her Olympic achievements. Only the third answer is general enough to be the main idea of the paragraph.

A main idea is also some kind of **assertion** about the subject. An assertion is a claim that something is true. Assertions can be facts or opinions, but in either case, an assertion should be supported by specific ideas, facts, and details. In other words, the main idea makes a general assertion that tells readers that something is true.

The supporting sentences, on the other hand, show readers that this assertion is true by providing specific facts and details. For example, in the Wilma Rudolph paragraph, the writer makes a general assertion: "Wilma Rudolph, the crippled child who became an Olympic running champion, is an inspiration for us all." The other sentences offer specific facts and details that prove why Wilma Rudolph is an inspirational person.

Writers often state their main ideas in one or two sentences so that readers can have a very clear understanding about the main point of the passage. A sentence that expresses the main idea of a paragraph is called a **topic sentence.**

Notice, for example, how the first sentence in the Wilma Rudolph paragraph states the main idea:

    "Wilma Rudolph, the crippled child who became an Olympic running champion, is an inspiration for us all."

This sentence is therefore the topic sentence for the paragraph. Topic sentences are often found at the beginning of paragraphs. Sometimes, though, writers begin with specific supporting ideas and lead up to the main idea, and in this case the topic sentence is often found at the end of the paragraph. Sometimes the topic sentence is even found somewhere in the middle, and other times there isn't a clear topic sentence at all—but that doesn't mean there isn't a main idea; the author has just chosen not to express it in a clear topic sentence. In this last case, you'll have to look carefully at the paragraph for clues about the main idea.

Main Ideas vs. Supporting Ideas

If you're not sure whether something is a main idea or a supporting idea, ask yourself the following question: is the sentence making a **general statement,** or is it providing **specific information?** In the Wilma Rudolph paragraph above, for example, all of the sentences except the first make specific statements. They are not general enough to serve as an umbrella or net for the whole paragraph.

Writers often provide clues that can help you distinguish between main ideas and their supporting ideas. Here are some of the most common words and phrases used to introduce specific examples:

1. **For example...**

2. **Specifically...**

3. **In addition...**

4. **Furthermore...**

5. **For instance...**

6. **Others...**

7. **In particular...**

8. **Some...**

These signal words tell you that a supporting fact or idea will follow. If you're having trouble finding the main idea of a paragraph, try eliminating sentences that begin with these phrases, because they will most likely be too specific to be a main ideas.

Implied Main Idea

When the main idea is **implied**, there's no topic sentence, which means that finding the main idea requires some detective work. But don't worry! You already know the importance of structure, word choice, style, and tone. Plus, you know how to read carefully to find clues, and you know that these clues will help you figure out the main idea.

For Example:

"One of my summer reading books was *The Windows of Time.* Though it's more than 100 pages long, I read it in one afternoon. I couldn't wait to see what happened to Evelyn, the main character. But by the time I got to the end, I wondered if I should have spent my afternoon doing something else. The ending was so awful that I completely forgot that I'd enjoyed most of the book."

There's no topic sentence here, but you should still be able to find the main idea. Look carefully at what the writer says and how she says it. What is she suggesting?

   a) *The Windows of Time* is a terrific novel.
   b) *The Windows of Time* is disappointing.
   c) *The Windows of Time* is full of suspense.
   d) *The Windows of Time* is a lousy novel.

The correct answer is **b)** – the novel is disappointing. How can you tell that this is the main idea? First, we can eliminate choice **c)**, because it's too specific to be a main idea. It deals only with one specific aspect of the novel (its suspense).

Sentences **a)**, **b)**, and **d)**, on the other hand, all express a larger idea – a general assertion about the quality of the novel. But only one of these statements can actually serve as a "net" for the whole paragraph. Notice that while the first few sentences praise the novel, the last two criticize it. Clearly, this is a mixed review.

Therefore, the best answer is **b)**. Sentence **a)** is too positive and doesn't account for the "awful" ending. Sentence **d)**, on the other hand, is too negative and doesn't account for the reader's sense of suspense and interest in the main character. But sentence **b)** allows for both positive and negative aspects – when a good thing turns bad, we often feel disappointed.

Now let's look at another example. Here, the word choice will be more important, so read carefully.

> "Fortunately, none of Toby's friends had ever seen the apartment where Toby lived with his mother and sister. Sandwiched between two burnt-out buildings, his two-story apartment building was by far the ugliest one on the block. It was a real eyesore: peeling orange paint (orange!), broken windows, crooked steps, crooked everything. He could just imagine what his friends would say if they ever saw this poor excuse for a building."

Which of the following expresses the main idea of this paragraph?

   a) Toby wishes he could move to a nicer building.
   b) Toby wishes his dad still lived with them.
   c) Toby is glad none of his friends know where he lives.
   d) Toby is sad because he doesn't have any friends.

From the description, we can safely assume that Toby doesn't like his apartment building and wishes he could move to a nicer building **a)**. But that idea isn't general enough to cover the whole paragraph, because it's about his building.

Because the first sentence states that Toby has friends, the answer cannot be **d)**. We know that Toby lives only with his mother and little sister, so we might assume that he wishes his dad still lived with them, **b)**, but there's nothing in the paragraph to support that assumption, and this idea doesn't include the two main topics of the paragraph—Toby's building and Toby's friends.

What the paragraph adds up to is that Toby is terribly embarrassed about his building, and he's glad that none of his friends have seen it **c)**. This is the main idea. The paragraph opens with the word "fortunately," so we know that he thinks it's a good thing none of his friends have been to his house. Plus, notice how the building is described: "by far the ugliest on the block," which says a lot since it's stuck "between two burnt-out buildings." The writer calls it an "eyesore," and repeats "orange" with an exclamation point to emphasize how ugly the color is. Everything is "crooked" in this "poor excuse for a building." Toby is clearly ashamed of where he lives and worries about what his friends would think if they saw it.

Cause and Effect

Understanding cause and effect is important for reading success. Every event has at least one cause (what made it happen) and at least one effect (the result of what happened). Some events have more than one cause, and some have more than one effect. An event is also often part of a chain of causes and effects. Causes and effects are usually signaled by important transitional words and phrases.

Words Indicating Cause:

1. **Because (of)**
2. **Created (by)**
3. **Caused (by)**
4. **Since**

Words Indicating Effect:

1. **As a result**
2. **Since**
3. **Consequently**
4. **So**
5. **Hence**
6. **Therefore**

Sometimes, a writer will offer his or her opinion about why an event happened when the facts of the cause(s) aren't clear. Or a writer may predict what he or she thinks will happen because of a certain event (its effects). If this is the case, you need to consider how reasonable those opinions are. Are the writer's ideas logical? Does the writer offer support for the conclusions he or she offers?

Reading Between the Lines

Paying attention to word choice is particularly important when the main idea of a passage isn't clear. A writer's word choice doesn't just affect meaning; it also creates it. For example, look at the following description from a teacher's evaluation of a student applying to a special foreign language summer camp.

There's no topic sentence, but if you use your powers of observation, you should be able to tell how the writer feels about her subject.

> "As a student, Jane usually completes her work on time and checks it carefully. She speaks French well and is learning to speak with less of an American accent. She has often been a big help to other students who are just beginning to learn the language."

What message does this passage send about Jane? Is she the best French student the writer has ever had? Is she one of the worst, or is she just average? To answer these questions, you have to make an inference, and you must support your inference with specific observations. What makes you come to the conclusion that you come to?

The **diction** of the paragraph above reveals that this is a positive evaluation, but not a glowing recommendation.

Here are some of the specific observations you might have made to support this conclusion:

- The writer uses the word "usually" in the first sentence. This means that Jane is good about meeting deadlines for work, but not great; she doesn't always hand in her work on time.

- The first sentence also says that Jane checks her work carefully. While Jane may sometimes hand in work late, at least she always makes sure it's quality work. She's not sloppy.

- The second sentence tells us she's "learning to speak with less of an American accent." This suggests that she has a strong accent and needs to improve in this area. It also suggests, though, that she is already making progress.

- The third sentence tells us that she "often" helps "students who are just beginning to learn the language." From this we can conclude that Jane has indeed mastered the basics. Otherwise, how could she be a big help to students who are just starting to learn? By looking at the passage carefully, then, you can see how the writer feels about her subject.

Test Your Knowledge: The Reading Section

Read each of the following paragraphs carefully and answer the questions that follow.

My "office" measures a whopping 5 x 7 feet. A large desk is squeezed into one corner, leaving just enough room for a rickety chair between the desk and the wall. Yellow paint is peeling off the walls in dirty chunks. The ceiling is barely six feet tall; it's like a hat that I wear all day long. The window, a single 2 x 2 pane, looks out onto a solid brick wall just two feet away.

1. What is the main idea implied by this paragraph?
    a) This office is small but comfortable.
    b) This office is in need of repair.
    c) This office is old and claustrophobic.
    d) None of the above.

There are many things you can do to make tax time easier. The single most important strategy is to keep accurate records. Keep all of your pay stubs, receipts, bank statements, and other relevant financial information in a neat, organized folder so that when you're ready to prepare your form, all of your paperwork is in one place. The second thing you can do is start early. Get your tax forms from the post office as soon as they are available and start calculating. This way, if you run into any problems, you have plenty of time to straighten them out. You can also save time by reading the directions carefully. This will prevent time-consuming errors. Finally, if your taxes are relatively simple (you don't have itemized deductions or special investments), use the shorter tax form. It's only one page, so if your records are in order, it can be completed in less than an hour.

2. How many suggestions for tax time does this passage offer?
    a) One.
    b) Two.
    c) Three.
    d) Four.

3. The sentence "It's only one page, so if your records are in order, it can be completed in less than an hour" is:
    a) The main idea of the passage.
    b) A major supporting idea.
    c) A minor supporting idea.
    d) A transitional sentence.

4. A good summary of this passage would be:
    a) Simple strategies can make tax time less taxing.
    b) Don't procrastinate at tax time.
    c) Always keep good records.
    d) Get a tax attorney.

5. According to the passage, who should use the shorter tax form?
    a) Everybody.
    b) People who do not have complicated finances.
    c) People who do have complicated finances.
    d) People who wait until the last minute to file taxes.

6. The sentence, "The single most important strategy is to keep accurate records," is a(n):
   a) Fact.
   b) Opinion.
   c) Both of the above.
   d) Neither of the above.

Being a secretary is a lot like being a parent. After a while, your boss becomes dependent upon you, just as a child is dependent upon his or her parents. Like a child who must ask permission before going out, you'll find your boss coming to you for permission, too. "Can I have a meeting on Tuesday at 3:30?" you might be asked, because you're the one who keeps track of your boss's schedule. You will also find yourself cleaning up after your boss a lot, tidying up papers and files the same way a parent tucks away a child's toys and clothes. And, like a parent protects his or her children from outside dangers, you will find yourself protecting your boss from certain "dangers"—unwanted callers, angry clients, and upset subordinates.

7. The main idea of this passage is:
   a) Secretaries are treated like children.
   b) Bosses treat their secretaries like children.
   c) Secretaries and parents have similar roles.
   d) Bosses depend too much upon their secretaries.

8. Which of the following is the topic sentence of the paragraph?
   a) Being a secretary is a lot like being a parent.
   b) After a while, your boss becomes dependent upon you, just as a child is dependent upon his or her parents.
   c) You will also find yourself cleaning up after your boss a lot, tidying up papers and files the same way a parent tucks away a child's toys and clothes.
   d) None of the above.

9. According to the passage, secretaries are like parents in which of the following ways?
   a) They make their bosses' lives possible.
   b) They keep their bosses from things that might harm or bother them.
   c) They're always cleaning and scrubbing things.
   d) They don't get enough respect.

10. This passage uses which point of view?
    a) First person.
    b) Second person.
    c) Third person.
    d) First and second person.

11. The tone of this passage suggests that:
    a) The writer is angry about how secretaries are treated.
    b) The writer thinks secretaries do too much work.
    c) The writer is slightly amused by how similar the roles of secretaries and parents are.
    d) The writer is both a secretary and a parent.

12. The sentence, "'Can't I have a meeting on Tuesday at 3:30?' you might be asked, because you're the one who keeps track of your boss's schedule," is a:
    a) Main idea.
    b) Major supporting idea.
    c) Minor supporting idea
    d) None of the above.

13. "Being a secretary is a lot like being a parent" is:
    a) A fact.
    b) An opinion.
    c) Neither of the above.
    d) Both of the above.

14. The word "subordinates" probably means:
    a) Employees.
    b) Parents.
    c) Clients.
    d) Secretaries.

Day after day, Johnny chooses to sit at his computer instead of going outside with his friends. A few months ago, he'd get half a dozen phone calls from his friends every night. Now, he might get one or two a week. It used to be that his friends would come over two or three days a week after school. Now, he spends his afternoons alone with his computer.

15. The main idea is:
    a) Johnny and his friends are all spending time with their computers instead of one another.
    b) Johnny's friends aren't very good friends.
    c) Johnny has alienated his friends by spending so much time on the computer.
    d) Johnny and his friends prefer to communicate by computer.

We've had Ginger since I was two years old. Every morning, she wakes me up by licking my cheek. That's her way of telling me she's hungry. When she wants attention, she'll weave in and out of my legs and meow until I pick her up and hold her. And I can always tell when Ginger wants to play. She'll bring me her toys and will keep dropping them (usually right on my homework!) until I stop what I'm doing and play with her for a while.

16. A good topic sentence for this paragraph would be:
    a) I take excellent care of Ginger.
    b) Ginger is a demanding pet.
    c) Ginger and I have grown up together.
    d) Ginger is good at telling me what she wants.

Test Your Knowledge: The Reading Section – Answers

1. c)
2. d)
3. c)
4. a)
5. b)
6. b)
7. c)
8. a)
9. b)
10. b)
11. c)
12. c)
13. b)
14. a)
15. c)
16. d)

Chapter 4: The Science Reasoning Section

The Science Reasoning section of the EXPLORE consists of seven groups of information (presented in passages, charts, tables, graphs, etc.), which cover multiple areas of science, such as astronomy, biology, chemistry, physics, earth, and life sciences.

Although you are not expected to have taken courses in all the subject areas covered, the EXPLORE does expect you to be able to use your reading comprehension and reasoning skills, as they apply, to the information you are given.

Some questions require you to understand contextual knowledge, expressions, basic facts, and theories about the information. Each passage is followed by several multiple-choice questions. Success is determined by your ability to quickly comprehend the information presented to you.

The information will be presented in three different formats:

- **Research Summaries:** Detailed narrative of one experiment or several correlated experiments.

- **Conflicting Viewpoints:** Multiple, differing theories about a scientific question.

- **The Data Representation:** Scientific information is presented in tables, graphs, or figures that summarize specific research.

Basic Skills Necessary

The science test requires you to: critically evaluate data and scientific arguments, recognize relationships, make generalizations, and draw conclusions. Be prepared to make simple mathematical calculations using the data. Some questions require you to understand background knowledge, terms, basic facts, and concepts about the information.

As with all the test sections, know the directions ahead of time.

Directions for the Science Reasoning Section:
Each of the seven passages in this test is followed by several questions. After you read each passage, select the correct choice for each of the questions that follow the passage. Refer to the passage as often as necessary to answer the questions. You may NOT use a calculator on this test.

General Tips

1. Refer to the passage for each question. Do not attempt to answer using your background knowledge or your memory of the passage. Answers are based on the data and information presented in the information given, not on what you did in a class.

2. You will have to work quickly. If you break it down, you have approximately five minutes to read each passage and answer the associated questions. Try to take only two or three minutes to study each passage. This will leave about twenty to thirty seconds for each of the questions.

3. Highlight the main points and other items which you feel are pertinent as you read.

4. During practice exams, try quickly skimming over the questions (but not the choices) before reading the passage, as well as the traditional read-and-answer, to see which works best for you. You may find that this approach is not only faster, but increases your percentage of correct answers by allowing you to focus on the key words in the questions.

5. Make sure you're answering the right question and referring to the right data set, hypothesis, or study.

Tips for Individual Formats

The following are tips for each of the different formats, along with the percentage of questions found on the test.

Research Summaries (45%)

1. The majority of the questions presented in the research summaries format require you to comprehend the purpose of the experiment.

2. Pay close attention to the experimental or study design, the methods used, and the results.

3. Be watchful for information or hypotheses which are not directly stated in the data that **may or may not** be drawn from the experiment.

4. Be able to recognize conclusions that can be drawn from the design of the study or experiment, as well as from the results.

5. Know how the data was obtained, retained, and displayed.

Conflicting viewpoints (17%)

1. Start by rereading the opening sentence of the passage to make sure that you know the scientific issues in dispute.

2. Recognize the main points of disagreement in the theories presented, since many of the *questions are based on these.* Try not to let the details of the given information interfere with recognizing the main points.

3. Focus on the key differences in the viewpoints, such as possible weaknesses in an argument and information that might strengthen or support a viewpoint.

4. Pay attention to additional information given in a question.

5. Keep in mind conflicts and contradictions; underlying assumptions in the viewpoints; as well as possible biases, and valid criticisms, of a viewpoint.

Data Representation (38%)

1. Focus on understanding what information is given.

2. Don't go by memory. Always refer to the visual representation (graph, chart, etc.) for each question.

3. Peruse the presented data carefully, looking for high and low points, as well as fluctuations and trends.

4. Review headings, factors, and/or descriptive facts given, noting the differences and correlations.

5. Pay attention to how the data is presented, such as how the terms are used in each representation (total, control, dependent, independent, etc.).

Test Your Knowledge: The Science Reasoning Section

The following passages will be followed by several questions. After you read each passage, select the correct choice for each of the questions that follow the passage. Refer to the passage as often as necessary to answer the questions. You may NOT use a calculator on this test.

Questions 1 – 6 are based on the following passages:

Asteroid-Impact Theory
The dinosaurs disappeared at the end of the Mesozoic era, about 65 million years ago. The disappearance took place over a very short period of time and was, according to some scientists, triggered by Earth colliding with a large asteroid.

Today, evidence of this collision can be found in the rock record. Geologists have discovered a thin layer of clay containing a high concentration of the element iridium between two particular rock layers. This boundary marks the end of the Mesozoic and the beginning of the Cenozoic era. This iridium-rich layer has been identified at the Mesozoic-Cenozoic boundary at many different locations around the world. Iridium, while rare on Earth, is a common substance in meteorites and asteroids.

The asteroid not only supplied the iridium, but its white-hot rock fragments also started fires that engulfed entire continents. The soot from these fires, combined with asteroid and crustal particles that were propelled into the atmosphere, blocked out the Sun's energy. The lack of sunlight halted photosynthesis and caused a decrease in global temperatures. Much of the plant and animal life, including the dinosaurs, could not adapt to the temperature change and died.

Gradual-Extinction Theory
Some scientists disagree with the asteroid-impact theory. They point to evidence which suggests that the dinosaurs died out gradually because of a long-term climatic change. Earth experienced increased volcanic activity 65 million years ago. This volcanism could have produced the iridium, but, more importantly, those volcanoes did produce tremendous amounts of carbon dioxide. The increased levels of carbon dioxide in the atmosphere prevented Earth from radiating excess heat back into space, and thus caused a worldwide warming.

The warming of Earth is what caused the dinosaurs' disappearance. After examining dinosaur egg fossils, paleontologists discovered that the eggshells became thinner in at least one species. This was thought to be the result of heat adversely affecting the dinosaurs' metabolism. These thin-shelled eggs, which were easily broken, lowered the survival rate among the offspring and contributed to the eventual extinction of the dinosaurs.

1. Astronomers recently estimated that only 3% of asteroids, with orbits that intersect Earth's, have been identified. This finding adds support to the asteroid impact theory by:
    a) Increasing the likelihood of past Earth-asteroid collisions.
    b) Showing how little astronomers know about asteroids.
    c) Proving that iridium-rich asteroids are common in the solar system.
    d) Showing that many asteroids are too small to be easily identified.

2. A geologist examines a sedimentary rock layer from the Mesozoic-Cenozoic boundary. According to the asteroid-impact theory, the geologist should not expect to find:
    a) A high concentration of iridium.
    b) A high concentration of soot particles.
    c) Evidence of great volcanic activity.
    d) Fossilized plant remains.

3. What do supporters of the asteroid-impact theory assume about the fires started by the white-hot asteroid fragments?
    a) They spread quickly and were wide-ranging.
    b) They removed carbon dioxide from the atmosphere, causing a global cooling.
    c) They burned the vegetation, limiting the food supply.
    d) They produced high levels of carbon dioxide, causing a global warming.

4. Both theories presented in the passage cite which of the following factors as contributing directly to the dinosaurs' extinction?
    a) High levels of soot and volcanic ash.
    b) High concentrations of iridium.
    c) Global temperature change.
    d) Increased amounts of carbon dioxide introduced into the atmosphere.

5. Mass extinctions throughout history often occur in conjunction with drops in the sea level. What would proponents of the gradual-extinction theory have to demonstrate in order to tie those facts together?
    a) Mass extinctions and drops in the sea level are both caused by increased volcanic activity.
    b) The greenhouse effect causes lowering of the sea level as well as gradual mass extinctions.
    c) With less water available, fires run rampant and destroy the food supply.
    d) Drops in the sea level and mass extinctions are caused by the same changes in climate.

6. After examining the 250-million-year fossil record, two paleontologists have uncovered evidence suggesting that the rate of species extinctions peaks every 26 million years. Supporters of the asteroid-impact theory would most likely favor which of the following explanations for this finding?
    a) Some massive object periodically disrupts the solar system, causing comets and asteroids to enter the inner solar system.
    b) The tilt of Earth's axis changes every 26 million years, causing long-term climatic changes which lead to mass-extinction episodes.
    c) Earth's orbit becomes more elliptical every 26 million years; and it travels farther from the Sun, which causes periods of global cooling.
    d) Earth's global weather patterns change in response to the size of the polar ice caps, plunging Earth into a global cooling pattern every 26 million years.

Questions 7 – 14 are based off the following information:

In chemistry, the flame test is a way of determining chemical compounds by observing the color of the resulting flame when a chemical reacts to heat. This test works particularly well with substances containing metal ions. An element's atoms, or a compound's molecules, emit a unique spectrum of color when altered to a lower energy state by heat. For example, the element Cu emits blue on the emission spectrum when exposed to heat.

Two students in a chemistry class are doing an experiment using the flame test. The students are given the following chart to complete:

Solution	Flame color
Barium (Ba)	
Calcium (Ca)	
Copper (Cu)	
Lead (Pb)	
Potassium (K)	
Sodium (Na)	
Strontium (Sr)	
Unknown solution #1	
Unknown solution #2	

The students complete the lab procedure. Using a clean test wire, they dip the wire into the first known solution: barium. They then hold the wire in the Bunsen burner flame. The students observe the color that the flame turns and note this on the chart. The students wait until the chemical burns off of the wire and the flame returns to normal, and then repeat the process for each of the known chemical solutions on the chart. They then test the unknown chemical solutions as well. Below are some of the results the students recorded:

Solution	Flame color
Barium (Ba)	Light green
Calcium (Ca)	Dark red
Copper (Cu)	
Lead (Pb)	White/blue
Potassium (K)	Light purple
Sodium (Na)	Bright orange
Strontium (Sr)	Bright orange/red
Unknown solution #1	
Unknown solution #2	

7. Which of the following colors should the students find the Copper solution emits?
   a) Purple.
   b) White.
   c) Bright yellow.
   d) Blue.

8. The teacher knows that Unknown solution #2 is simply a Barium solution. What color should students record in their flame charts for Unknown solution #2 to receive full credit?
   a) Light green.
   b) Blue.
   c) Bright red.
   d) Bright orange.

9. The flame test may not be a useful way to determine a chemical solution for all of the following reasons except that:
   a) Some solutions emit similar colors on the spectrum and are hard to distinguish.
   b) It might be more difficult to determine the identity of a mixed solution.
   c) A contained flame is not always available.
   d) The color emitted by different chemicals can change over time.

10. The lab instructor informs the students that they have filled in the wrong color for Strontium – the solution is supposed to be orange, not an orange/red. Which of the following is likely the source of the students' error?
    a) The students are both unable to distinguish between red and orange.
    b) The students accidentally switched two of the test tubes containing their solutions.
    c) The students failed to let all of the Sodium solution burn off while testing the previous solution, so the test wire had both solutions on it.
    d) The students misread the solution names on the chart.

11. The students find that Unknown solution #1 is white/blue. Which of the following is the likely metal compound in the solution?
    a) Barium.
    b) Calcium.
    c) Copper.
    d) Lead.

12. The students learn that fireworks emit bright colors through the use of different chemical compounds. If a fireworks producer wanted to create a red firework, which of the following metals should be added to the compound?
    a) Lead.
    b) Calcium.
    c) Copper.
    d) Potassium.

13. What color flame would the students expect to record if they dipped a test wire in a solution containing an alloy of Cu and Pb?
    a) Light blue.
    b) Dark blue.
    c) White.
    d) Purple.

14. Scientists have used the unique color spectrum of elements to determine new elements. The discoveries of each of the following elements illustrates this strategy EXCEPT:
    a) The discovery of Radium in 1898 by extracting the chemical compound from a uranium sample and distinguishing the brilliant green flame color of barium from the unknown compound's crimson color spectrum.
    b) The discovery of eka-caesium in 1939 by examining the decay product energy levels in a sample of actinium-227/
    c) The discovery of Gallium in 1871 spectroscopically by examining its unique violet spectrum in a sample of Sphalerite.
    d) The discovery of Helium in 1868 by examining the wavelength of the elements burning in the chromosphere of the Sun.

Questions 15 – 20 are based off the following information:

The coffee plant, *Coffea*, is a flowering plant whose seeds, coffee beans, are used to brew the beverage coffee. Coffee beans are a major export for many developing countries, and thus the best conditions in which to grow the coffee plant have been rigorously studied. The best *Coffea* is generally grown in the "coffee belt" – the region around the globe which is within ten degrees latitude of the equator. There are many different species of the plant with slightly different optimal growing conditions. Below are the results of two studies on the best conditions for growing *Coffea arabica*.

Study I
Coffea arabica is planted in four fields at different elevations. The plants are left to mature for seven years, and then the beans are harvested. Yields of the harvests are recorded. Coffee is brewed using the same technique with beans from each of the four fields, and the resulting coffee is given a rating which ranges from Poor, to Fair, to Good, to Excellent by professional coffee "Master Tasters." Below are the results from this study:

Elevation above sea level	Bean Yield	Coffee Rating
500 m	120 kg	Fair
1000 m	350 kg	Excellent
1700 m	600 kg	Good
2200 m	400 kg	Poor

Study II
Different types of *Coffea arabica* have been found to produce different levels of caffeine in their beans. A corporation looking to produce a high-quality, low-caffeine strain of coffee commissioned a study to determine which factors result in low caffeine-producing beans. The firm conducting the study ran a comparison of different strains of *Coffea arabica* found across the globe. A table detailing this comparison is found below:

Strain	Elevation grown (altitude)	Latitude grown	Percent caffeine
1	500 m	10° N	4%
2	1200 m	4° S	5%
3	1200 m	0° (Equatorial)	5.5%
4	1700 m	8° S	4%
5	1700 m	5° N	6%

15. If the corporation which commissioned Study II makes a decision solely based on the results of this study, which coffee strain will they decide to produce?
    a) 1.
    b) 1 and/or 3.
    c) 5.
    d) 4 and/or 1.

16. If the corporation which commissioned Study II also incorporated data from Study I, which strain of *Coffea arabica* might they decide to grow?
    a) 1.
    b) 2.
    c) 3.
    d) 4.

17. Which of the following is a possible correlation between altitude at which *Coffea arabica* is grown and the resulting quality of the coffee brewed?
    a) *Coffea arabica* grown at higher altitudes produces better coffee.
    b) *Coffea arabica* grown at higher altitudes produces worse coffee.
    c) The best coffee is produced by growing *Coffea arabica* at either very low or very high altitudes.
    d) The best coffee is produced by growing *Coffea arabica* between altitudes of 1000-2000 m.

18. Which of the following is possibly correlated with caffeine content of a coffee bean?
    a) The elevation at which the coffee plant was grown.
    b) The latitude at which the coffee plant was grown.
    c) The quality of the coffee brewed with the bean.
    d) None of these are correlated with caffeine content.

19. A coffee producer is using the results of only Study I to determine the best location to grow coffee, and wants to maximize first yield and then quality. At which elevation should the coffee producer plant *Coffea arabica*?
    a) 500 m.
    b) 1000 m.
    c) 1700 m.
    d) 2200 m.

20. Which of the following may have been an untested variable which impacted the results of Study I?
    a) The technique used to brew coffee with the beans of each of the four fields.
    b) The quality of the soil in each of the four fields.
    c) The elevation at which the plants were grown.
    d) The species of coffee plant grown.

Test Your Knowledge: The Science Reasoning Section – Answers

1. a)
2. c)
3. a)
4. c)
5. d)
6. a)
7. d)
8. a)
9. d)
10. c)
11. d)
12. b)
13. a)
14. b) All the others give examples of using spectrum testing.
15. d)
16. d) Strain 4 has a low caffeine percentage and is grown at a latitude associated with high yields and good quality.
17. d)
18. d)
19. c)
20. b) All other variables are either explicitly tested or explicitly held constant.

<u>Final Thoughts</u>

In the end, we know that you will be successful in taking the EXPLORE. Although the road ahead may at times be challenging, if you continue your hard work and dedication (just like you are doing to prepare right now!), you will find that your efforts will pay off.

If you are struggling after reading this book and following our guidelines, we sincerely hope that you will take note of our advice and seek additional help. Start by asking friends about the resources that they are using. If you are still not reaching the score you want, consider getting the help of a tutor.

If you are on a budget and cannot afford a private tutoring service, there are plenty of independent tutors, including college students who are proficient in the tested subjects. You don't have to spend thousands of dollars to afford a good tutor or review course.

We wish you the best of luck and happy studying. Most importantly, we hope you enjoy your coming years – after all, you put a lot of work into getting there in the first place.

Sincerely,
The Trivium Team